W9-AOY-263

Zoo Animals

Kangaroo

Patricia Whitehouse

Heinemann Library
Chicago, Illinois

Customer Service 888-454-2279
Visit our website at www.heinemannlibrary.com

Designed by Sue Emerson, Heinemann Library
Printed and bound in the United States by Lake Book Manufacturing, Inc.

07 06 05 04 03
10 9 8 7 6 5 4 3 2 1

Library of Congress Cataloging-in-Publication Data
Whitehouse, Patricia, 1958-
        Kangaroo / Patricia Whitehouse.
            p. cm. — (Zoo animals)
Includes index.
Summary: An introduction to kangaroos, describing their size, diet and everyday life style and
highlighting differences between those in the wild and those living in a zoo habitat.
        ISBN: 1-58810-889-9 (HC), 1-40340-545-X (Pbk.)
        1. Kangaroos—Juvenile literature. [1. Kangaroos. 2. Zoo animals.] I. Title.
        QL737.M35 W45 2002
        599.2'22—dc21

                        2001008040

Acknowledgments
The author and publishers are grateful to the following for permission to reproduce copyright material:
Title page, p. 7 John Cancalosi/DRK Photo; pp. 4, 22, 24 Charles Philip/Visuals Unlimited; p. 5 Roland Seitre/Peter
Arnold, Inc.; p. 6 Inga Spence/Visuals Unlimited; pp. 8, 9, 19, 20 Mitsuaki Iwago/Minden Pictures; p. 10 Walt
Anderson/Visuals Unlimited; pp. 11, 15 Chicago Zoological Society/The Brookfield Zoo; p. 12 Frans Lanting/Minden
Pictures; p. 13 Jim Schulz/Chicago Zoological Society/The Brookfield Zoo; pp. 14, 21 Martin Harvey/DRK Photos; p. 16
antphoto.com.au; p. 17 Tom Brakefield/Corbis; p. 18 Steve Kaufman/Corbis; p. 23 (row 1, L-R) Chicago Zoological
Society/The Brookfield Zoo, Frans Lanting/Minden Pictures, Lawrence M. Sawyer/PhotoDisc; p. 23 (row 2, L-R) Jim
Schulz/Chicago Zoological Society/The Brookfield Zoo, Mitsuaki Iwago/Minden Pictures, John Cancalosi/DRK Photo;
p. 23 (row 3, L-R) Jack Ballard/Visuals Unlimited, John Cancalosi/DRK Photo, Jim Schulz/Chicago Zoological Society/
The Brookfield Zoo; back cover (L-R) Charles Philip/Visuals Unlimited, Martin Harvey/DRK Photos

Cover photograph by Martin Harvey/DRK Photos
Photo research by Bill Broyles

Every effort has been made to contact copyright holders of any material reproduced in this book.
Any omissions will be rectified in subsequent printings if notice is given to the publisher.

Special thanks to our advisory panel for their help in the preparation of this book:

Eileen Day, Preschool Teacher
Chicago, IL

Ellen Dolmetsch,
Library Media Specialist
Wilmington, DE

Kathleen Gilbert,
Teacher
Round Rock, TX

Sandra Gilbert,
Library Media Specialist
Houston, TX

Angela Leeper,
Educational Consultant
North Carolina Department
of Public Instruction
Raleigh, NC

Pam McDonald, Reading Teacher
Winter Springs, FL

Melinda Murphy,
Library Media Specialist
Houston, TX

We would also like to thank Lee Haines, Assistant Director of Marketing and Public Relations at the Brookfield Zoo
in Brookfield, Illinois, for his review of this book.

Some words are shown in bold, **like this.**
You can find them in the picture glossary on page 23.

Contents

What Are Kangaroos?

pouch

Kangaroos are **marsupials.**

Marsupials are animals that carry their babies in a **pouch.**

In the wild, kangaroos live where
it is warm all year.

But you can see kangaroos at
the zoo.

What Do Kangaroos Look Like?

ears

tail

Kangaroos have long ears and a long tail.

They have brown or gray hair.

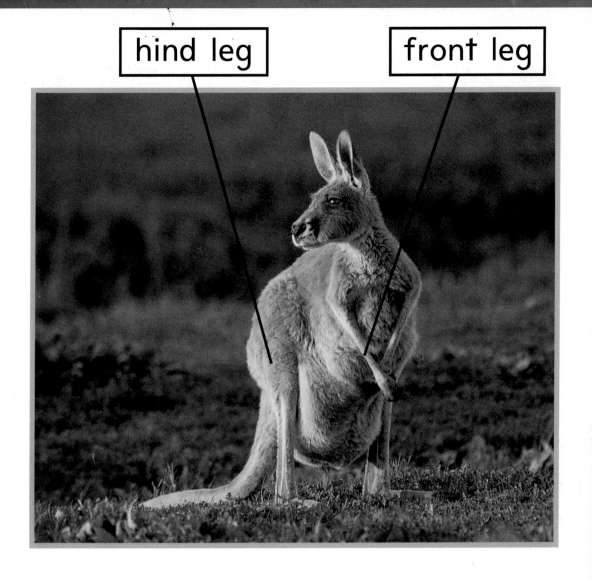

hind leg

front leg

Kangaroos have long **hind legs.**

They have short front legs.

What Do Baby Kangaroos Look Like?

Baby kangaroos are called **joeys.**

New joeys are the size of a bean!

At first, joeys have no hair.

They stay in their mother's **pouch** while they grow.

Where Do Kangaroos Live?

In the wild, some kangaroos live in **grasslands**.

Some live in forests.

In the zoo, kangaroos live in large **enclosures**.

Grasses and other plants grow there.

What Do Kangaroos Eat?

In the wild, kangaroos eat grass and small plants.

At the zoo, kangaroos eat **hay** and **grains.**

Zookeepers also feed them fruit.

13

What Do Kangaroos Do All Day?

In the wild, kangaroos sleep most of the day.

A mother and her **joey** sleep in the shade.

At the zoo, kangaroos are awake most of the day.

They spend the day eating and resting.

What Do Kangaroos Do at Night?

In the wild, kangaroos are nocturnal.

They look for food at night.

At the zoo, kangaroos sleep at night.

They do not have to find food.

What Sounds Do Kangaroos Make?

Kangaroos can make a soft chirping noise.

They make this noise when they see other animals.

Kangaroos can also growl.

They growl when they are in danger.

How Are Kangaroos Special?

Kangaroos use their strong tails to balance.

They sometimes balance on their tails when they play.

Kangaroos are good jumpers.

A kangaroo could jump across your classroom in two jumps!

Quiz

Do you remember what a baby kangaroo is called?

Look for the answer on page 24.

?

Picture Glossary

enclosure
page 11

hind leg
page 7

nocturnal
page 16

grain
page 13

joey
pages 8, 9, 14

pouch
pages 4, 9

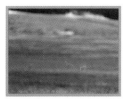

grasslands
page 10

marsupial
page 4

zookeeper
page 13

hay
page 13

Note to Parents and Teachers

Reading for information is an important part of a child's literacy development. Learning begins with a question about something. Help children think of themselves as investigators and researchers by encouraging their questions about the world around them. In this book, the animal is identified as a marsupial. Marsupials are animals that have a pouch in which they nurse and carry their young. The symbol for marsupial in the picture glossary shows a female kangaroo carrying a joey in her pouch. The symbol for pouch shows the exterior of a kangaroo's pouch with the joey's head protruding. Explain to children that although kangaroos have the most easily identified pouches, other animals—such as opossums—are marsupials, too.

Index

Answers to quiz on page 22

A baby kangaroo is called a joey.

24